Life Love and the Lord

David D Kush

iUniverse, Inc.
New York   Bloomington

Life Love and the Lord

iUniverse books may be ordered through booksellers or by contacting:

iUniverse
1663 Liberty Drive
Bloomington, IN 47403
www.iuniverse.com
1-800-Authors (1-800-288-4677)

Because of the dynamic nature of the Internet, any Web addresses or links contained in this book may have changed since publication and may no longer be valid. The views expressed in this work are solely those of the author and do not necessarily reflect the views of the publisher, and the publisher hereby disclaims any responsibility for them.

ISBN: 978-1-4401-1922-4 (sc)
ISBN: 978-1-4401-1923-1 (ebook)

Printed in the United States of America

iUniverse rev. date: 6/29/2009

Contents

A Rose 1

My Cousin and Me 2

I Choose 3

Let Me Soar 4

A Letter from Kiwi 5

I Miss 6

Letter To Myself 7

Amazing Grace 8

As I See It 9

Joyfully 10

Look in the Mirror 11

Attempted 12

Breath 13

Cast in Stone 14

Death 15

Depression 16

Dreams 17

Falling Leaves 18

For Me 19

Forever Friend 20

Going Home 21

Good-bye 22

I Choose 23

I Will Fight 24

I Wonder. 25

If You See Me. 26

In the Shadow. 27

Just a Man 28

Life 29

Life Hands You 30

Life's Dance 31

Lose to Win. 32

Love—Pass It On 33

Maybe Tomorrow 34

MC3 35

Morning. 36

Mountain Snows. 37

My Heart Is Full 38

November Skies. 39

Oh, Just to Go Back 40

Oh, That Tree 41

One Rule 42

One Tiny Teardrop .43

Rebirth 44

Stand 45

Stood Up. 46

Take a Closer Look. 47

Tears from Heaven. 48

The Book 49

Power of One 50

These Words 51

My Sister. 52

Unmatched Beauty. 53

What Is Love. 54

Where Does It Go. 55

Where's God. 56

Winner at Last 57

Words Never Spoken 58

You Are Special to Me 59

You Were There 60

My Christmas Wish. 61

Waiting 62

Black and White 63

Forever Seventeen. 64

Time Machine. 65

True Love Is 66

The Greatest Surgeon 67

Forgiveness 68

God's Given Me Two 69

Never Let 70

Love Echoes. 71

Life Seasons. 72

My Goal 73

For Me 74

Believe 75

GPS 76

When We Were Young 77

Look in the Mirror 78

Temptress 79

No Plan 80

My Cousin and Me 81

Shadow Caster 82

One of a Kind 83

We All 84

The Lord Is Coming 85

A Song 86

A Rose

When some people think of a rose, they see a flower.
When I do, I see a friend.
She always has her heart out to help someone,
Many times getting hurt in the end.
That doesn't seem to stop her.
For people like her are very rare.
For many when there's no one to turn to
There is Rose standing there.
Oh, how better the world would be
If all became a Rose.

My Cousin and Me

You're more than a cousin to me.
All these years you've been a big part of me.
God's made us closer than most, and I thank him, of course.
For without you, I might not be me.
For you've always been there,
Showing me how much you care
When life's not been very kind to me.
So I hope and I pray that God blesses you every day,
The way you've been a blessing to me.

I Choose

To you who saved my life.
I choose for you to be happy
Were the words given to me.
These seven short words were the words that set me free.
Just when I thought no one cared,
These seven words showed me somebody was there.
They raised me out of depression,
Brought me back to life.
For these seven small words,
I will owe you the rest of my life.

Let Me Soar.

Lord, let me soar with the eagles
So I may see what you see.
Let me look down at the earth
To see what the people need.
Love, peace, and harmony are at your command.
Lord, won't please restore these gifts
Throughout every land.
Let the people on the earth
Feel what life could be
If, instead of their fighting,
Living in harmony.
Then putting all that effort
That was wasted in making war
Into making everyone's life better.
For now and evermore.

A Letter from Kiwi

Don't wake me up to say good-bye.
All it would do is make us both cry.
My time here on this earth was really good.
You took me in when no one else would.
The love you showed me was understood.
That God's people help even the lowliest creatures of the earth.
May God bless you for all you do.
For I and Louie are waiting for you.

I Miss

I miss the closeness we used to know,
The kind that we had not so long ago.
I thought that time would bring it back
Now that the kids are gone.
I guess that I was really wrong.
For it seems the old feelings are all but gone.
Oh, how did we let them get away?
Maybe those feelings only come
When things are new and we were young
And we never let life get in our way.

LETTER TO MYSELF

I really didn't see it coming,
The pain I put you through.
All those lonely nights
When I wasn't there for you.
I can feel the pent-up anger,
The hate that's consuming you.
I guess I lost my chance at heaven
By the hell I put you through.
If we could start all over again,
Would we feel the same?
Or would the past kill any chance
Of ending any other way?
I don't know what to tell you.
I don't know what to say.
But one thing I know for certain:
Tomorrow brings a brand new day.

Amazing Grace

Oh, how sweet the sun upon my face.
I thank the Lord for his amazing grace,
For what I have been given upon this earth,
And for what I know awaits me when I return to dirt.
I know his love is everlasting.
So I'm thanking all those who I met along the way,
Helping me make it through my day.
For that is why God put us on this earth:
To be like him while he's away,
To bring a little hope and happiness to all each day.

As I See It

Look, but look, past the obvious.
Listen and hear the unspoken words.
Give comfort to those that are hurting.
Open your life to those who are lonely.
Never stop dreaming for dreamers never grow old.
Loosen your grip on yesterday
So you can grab hold of today.
Go with your gut feeling,
For nine times out of ten
It's the right thing to do.
Laugh for laugher lifts the soul.
Give some time for helping others
For in the end it will help you.
Make something your passion
For without one, life is dull.
Thank all those who have helped you along the way.
Never let life harden your heart
For love now, past, or future makes life bearable.
Last of all; thank the Lord for he has made it all possible.

Joyfully

When I was drowning in a sea of darkness
The Lord sent me a light.
And the light that he sent me was
JOYFULLY ... JOYFULLY.
I thought the Lord had abandoned me.
Why, I didn't know.
So he sent me an angel to tell me
That it wasn't so.
And the angel he sent me was
JOYFULLY ... JOYFULLY.
She told me that he loved me,
That he would never let me go.
Just turn back to the Father.
That he he'd make me whole .
Now I thank the Lord for sending me
JOYFULLY ... JOYFULLY.

When I was drowning in a sea of darkness.

Look in the Mirror

Look in the mirror and you will see
The person in the mirror
Is a lot like me,
Hearing about your life and who you turned out to be.
Sometimes it sounds you're talking not about you
But you're talking about me.
Funny how alike we are in so many ways.
Too bad we didn't see it back in the old days.
Maybe we could have bypassed some of the pain.
I used to pray the Lord is my shepherd and didn't know why.
You opened my eyes
To see I was always part of his flock.
For You are my blessing and *you* are my rock

Attempted

I felt so lost and alone
That I ran into the arms of death.
And even she didn't want me.

Breath

God is only one breath away.
So breathe deep.
And use each breath wisely.

Cast in Stone

Some things are written in stone
Long before we're known.
Cast by the hand of God
For his words are so inspiring
Of who we turn out to be.
Sometimes it takes a lifetime
To realize where we are going.
So never doubt his reasons
Of where you are in life
For one day you'll be shown
When all things will come to light
That we are here for a purpose,
Of who and what we'll be.
So take a look back in time
At the path you have taken
For it's the one that was always meant to be.

Death

Death does not come easily.
It takes a lifetime to achieve.

Depression

I look but do not see.
I listen but do not hear.
I want to do but I can't.
There is hurt but no pain.
It is day, but I can't see the light
For my life is full of darkness.
I eat but do not hunger.
I am in a crowd, but I still feel alone.
Life is drained away, leaving nothing but a shell.

Dreams

Why do we dream anyway?
Is it an escape from everyday life?
It's like having a life not possible in light,
Being something we could never be.
Is it a look at the future
Or a past that we would like to change?
So inside of me is the world I can be,
Anything my heart delights.
I can have anything I ever wanted:
Rewrite what has happened in the past,
Making our lives perfect.
Even if it's only for one night.

Falling Leaves

We are but leaves on the tree of life,
Surrounded by family and friends most of our life.
As the seasons change, they begin to fall,
Sometimes leaving us alone till it's our time to fall.
I hope the Lord's rake is big enough that
We'll all be in the same pile.

For Me

In you I find peace,
A safe place to be.
When the world is going crazy,
I know you're with me.
For you are the rock,
The rock that stands against the raging sea.
You gave me a purpose
In what I was to be.
When I was captured by life's troubles,
You set me free.
I am starting to see my part
To help all who come my way,
The ones who are in need the most
To feel your healing heart.
Now the life I know
Is to give my life to thee.
For you, my Lord,
Stretched out your arms on the cross for me.

Forever Friend

Seems you've been there forever,
Since we were just kids—
Me with that goofy look,
You with that special grin.
Oh, how the years have gone before us,
Going our separate ways.
For God's reasons
Through all these many seasons,
He brings us back together
Every now and then.
To touch each other's lives,
Trying to stop the hurts,
Making all the wrongs right.
I don't know his reasons,
But I thank him every night
For it makes life bearable
To still have you part of my life.

Going Home

I went to where you lay today.
Stood there staring at the ground.
It seems like only yesterday
When you were still around.
Funny oh how much time has passed.
Yet those memories of you just don't seem to fade.
So someday we will meet again
When I, too, am in the grave.

Good-bye

You know we never really said good-bye.
Maybe because you didn't want to make me cry
About a love I thought was true.
I guess it wasn't real for you.
But after all these years,
I can still look into your eyes
To see a friendship that will never die.

I Choose

I choose for you to be happy
Were the words given to me.
These seven short words were the words that set me free.
Just when I thought no one cared,
These seven words showed me that I was wrong.
They raised me out of depression,
Brought me back to life.
For these seven small words,
I will owe you the rest of my life.

I Will Fight

I will fight the good fight for as long as I can.
And when the day's over, I can still call myself a man.
You may try to intimidate me and nitpick me too,
But at the end of each day,
I can honestly say I gave my best to you.
I'm sorry my God gave me higher morals than you.
So that's what I am; there's nothing you can do.
So next time you come looking for me, I'll show you no fear
For I have the *big man* backing me.
Ultimately, you may win on what you call this earth,
But my goal is heaven,
And not this piece of dirt.

I Wonder

Sometimes I sit and wonder
How things might have been
If I wasn't with her,
You weren't with him.
Would our lives be different, or would they be the same?
Making the only difference
The way you spell your last name.
Would all of life's troubles
Change the way we feel,
Taking what was once special,
Making it no big deal.
Funny how life can do that to you.
You just let it slip away,
Waking up one morning,
Agreeing to go your separate ways.

If You See Me

If you see me crying,
It's because our love is dying.
There's nothing I can do.
I've tried time and time to save it,
But I get no response from you.
It seems all you've ever wanted is to have your dreams come true.
If that's the case,
I've lost the race, and this is good-bye to you.

In the Shadow

If you walk in the shadow of the Lord,
You will never know the warmth
Of his son.

Just a Man

The Lord is always listening,
Waiting for my call.
He's always there next to me
If I stumble and fall.
With outstretched arms he picks me up
For he understands
That though I was made in his image,
I'm just a man.

Life

Life is God polishing
The apple within.
That's where real beauty lies—
In the soul.
For that's all that is left
When we come before our maker.

Life Hands You

Sometimes life hands you a lot of crap
Before you have the paper to clean it up.

Life's Dance

Sometimes you have to take a chance
If you want to dance
At the party they call life.
If you never try
You'll wonder why
Everyone is going right past.
For all you have to do
Is nothing new—
Take that first step.

Lose to Win

Sometimes you have to lose to win.
You lose a lover but gain a friend.
Oh, how lucky I have been.
For love can be lost, but friendships
Need never end.
So when in life you least expect it,
A friendship thought lost is resurrected
Out of the blue so unexpected.
Just when you need it most.

Love—Pass It On

Love is something special,
Something we should show,
Not holding back.
But giving it a chance to grow,
If we didn't hide it,
By helping our fellow man,
Then the world would know.
That loving one another
Would spread peace throughout the land.

Maybe Tomorrow

Sometimes it hurts to say good-bye.
It might even make you cry.
You might think it's the end.
You never know when
Life will join you again.
So until then, my friend,
Back in that special place you will go,
Where God only knows
When we might meet again.

MC3

Welcome God's children to MC3.
Walk through the doors and you will see
What great things God can do.
With open arms we welcome you.
For we are God's children, and you are too.
We'll feed your soul and give you respect,
Fill your heart with love,
Where there was once neglect.
So sit down and have coffee or tea,
Donuts or bagels, they are all free.
There will also be a box of food waiting for you
For that's only part of what we can do.
For inside these walls, God comes alive.
His outstretched arms are open so wide
To help you find his love and grace
For we are of the same family—the human race.
And that is why we care deeply about you.
For that is what God wants us all to do.

Morning

I love the stillness of morning
For that's when I can hear God breathe life into a new day.

Mountain Snows

Like the melting mountain snows
Bringing life to the valleys below,
May your healing waters
Pass over me to renew my faith
In Jesus Christ once again
So I may live in him, for him,
To proclaim his everlasting love
For all of mankind.
Let me be a light in the dark
For all who have lost their way,
Showing all he cares.

My Heart Is Full

My heart is full of fire.
It's burning with desire
To hear your word, oh Lord.
Your words they do amaze me.
They lift me and drive me crazy,
Giving me the truth
To who you really are.
For you are the answer
To all the world's cancers.
Your words forever echo in my heart.
You give me understanding
In a world that's so demanding.
That without you, Lord,
I'm nothing at all.

November Skies

Oh, how I hate these cold and dark November skies.
The gloom outside starts to creep inside,
Killing off all the joy that I once knew,
Wondering what's keeping me alive,
Trying to find a reason to survive.
All these days and nights of loneliness,
Maybe there are none at all.
Might this be my last call?
If it is, I give my thanks to all that cared
And all who gave a damn.

Oh, Just to Go Back

Oh, just to go back for just one day
When I had an imagination and knew how to play,
Where life troubles never got in the way.
Everything was taken care of by Mom and Pop.
They always knew what was needed and what was not.
I know I wasn't rich.
Never realized I was poor.
For the world was mine when I went out the front door.
All I had to do was close my eyes,
Then my imagination took over, and the world became my prize.

Oh, That Tree

Maybe if you would have seen
Our initials carved in that tree,
Maybe you might have fallen in love with me
When we were so very young.
For I wanted all the world to know
How I felt about you.
Now, after thirty years,
I went back to that tree
To see if I could still see
If those words could be seen.
Looking there, to my surprise,
Two words carved right next to mine:
I KNOW

One Rule

I went to talk to God today
For I thought it was time for me to go.
He told me that my work on earth wasn't quite through
For he had many more things for me to do.
There are many people that need your help
To make it through their day.
By helping them you're helping me.
My grace will come to you
For you're my answer to their prayers.
This I'm telling you.
For when all people realize this,
My gates will be open to you.

One Tiny Teardrop

One tiny teardrop
Rolling down my face.
One tiny teardrop
Seems so out of place.
I've tried and tried to stop it.
There's nothing more I can do.
For that one tiny teardrop
Was all I had left for you.
I'm just tired of all the trying
To keep from leaving you.
For that was the last tiny teardrop
I'm going to shed because of you.

Rebirth

Lord, let your waters wash over me,
Releasing me from the person I used to be.
For I have heard your word.
Now it lives in me.
Lord, raise me up.
Take me home.
Set me free.

Stand

Sometimes you have to take a stand.
And sometimes you have to stand alone.
But when you stand alone, people can see who you are
And what you stand for.

Stood Up

In a sea of friends and family,
You stood up for me.
When I was at my lowest point in life,
You brought life back to me.
That is why I laid down that stone.
For the word that was written on it
Reminded me of you.
It was the very least
That I could do for you.
Some day, when you look at it,
Remember the life you saved.
For everything you said to me
Kept me from an early grave.

Take a Closer Look

Sometimes a person's life isn't what it seems to be.
When you're on the outside looking in,
All you see is what's on the surface,
Never the turmoil that's being held within
If you were allowed to take a look inside,
To see the real truth.
We all should be glad of who we are,
Never being jealous, envious, or hurt.
For everyone has burdens,
No matter how great or how small.
For no one gets away that easy
Till they pass through heaven's door.

Tears from Heaven

Teardrops from heaven
Are what make the flowers grow.
This is their gift to all of us who are left here below.
Tears of gladness, not of sadness, are what they are indeed.
For they wait for us in heaven.
Where all are intended to be.

The Book

I went to the top of the mountain
To see what I could see.
Looking toward the heavens, I saw God looking back at me.
He asked me what I was doing there
So high up in the sky.
I said I was looking for the meaning to life
Before it was time to die.
He said all the answers I'd come to seek
Were written inside the book.
They have been there forever
For those who believe enough to look.

Power of One

The power of one can be awesome
If it's believing in the power of his Son.
When all the world's religions come to realize this,
The world will unite as one.
Together they will stop all the misery,
Bring happiness to the earth.
For this is his plan for all of us:
To bring heaven down to the earth.

These Words

These words that flow from my fingertips
Come from a place I try to forget
Called loneliness.
These words they create a comfort to me,
Expressing the person I wish to be.
In a world of my own,
Where love and happiness surround me.
Not in this I was born to be.
Someday the Lord will set me free.
I await that day.

My Sister

thank you
I know we're brother and sister.
We fell from the same family tree.
Never realized we had so much in common
Till you came to rescue me.
Never before have we talked so much.
It's good to know you are there.
For when I look at you,
It's almost like looking at me.
May you always remember
I'll owe you the rest of my life.
If you weren't my sister,
I'd ask you to be my wife.

Unmatched Beauty

With no pencil, paper, or brush in hand,
The Lord has painted a picture for every man.
Everything upon the earth
Came alive with every stroke of his mighty hand.
No one on earth can copy his work
For he is the master, the author of the book.

What Is Love

As the power of the sun warms the earth,
Love sets the heart on fire.
Like a breath of fresh air,
It revives the soul.
For as the warm spring rains
Wash away the last dirty snows of winter,
Love clears away old hurts,
Pain of lost love,
Bringing hope and a new beginning once again.

Where Does It Go

Where does a love go when it says good-bye?
Where does a love go when it starts to die?
I tried and tried to save it,
But all I can do is cry.
Where does a love go when it's no longer found inside?
How did it escape me?
I will never know.
I thought if I tried hard enough
It would start to grow.
But when I woke up this morning,
There was nothing left inside.
So can anyone tell me
Where a love goes when it withers and dies?

Where's God

Why do we turn our eyes to heaven
When GOD is found within?

Winner at Last

I guess it really was never meant to be—
Being more than friends you and me.
Looking back at all the years,
Why it never happened it may never be known.
Once or twice getting so close.
Always thinking it was a loss.
Now I realize I came out on top.
For we are close friends even today.
I know some people may never understand
How what we have could be so grand.
That knowing you the way I do
Made me a better person in all I do.
For you always brought out the best in me.
I hope someday you can say that too.
That knowing me in some way did something special for you.

Words Never Spoken

Seems that words that are never spoken
Are the ones we remember most.
For they are the words we wanted to say
To someone we held so very close.
Always on the tip of our tongue
But never slipping out.
If only we had the courage to say
What was in our hearts,
Maybe the world would be a better place.
Or a beginning to a brand-new start.

You Are Special to Me

After all these years,
It amazes me that you could still care,
To put my life ahead of yours.
For you know what could come about
If he would find out.
For I know he would never understand
That a woman and a man .
Can be just good friends.
You came into my life
Long before you became his wife.
I respect him as your husband and your life,
But I will never forget you.
You'll always be special to me.
For part of you was made part of me
So very long ago
That I tried and I can't let go.
You're deep inside my soul.
I thank the Lord above
For who you are.

You Were There

You were there just a short time.
You were there to set me free
From the depths of depression.
You were there to heal me.
I reached out and you touched me
In a way no one else will ever see.
Oh, the years have come between us,
But the heart that God gave you
Gave you the compassion to rescue me.
Oh, I wish the world was a little different,
Where friends could be just friends.
For there are too many questions that need answers,
Answers that can only come from a trusted friend.
For who else is more trusting
Than those who put others first.
If the Bible was written tomorrow,
Your name would appear in bold print.
For truly, you are one of God's people.
One I will never forget.

My Christmas Wish

Oh, Lord, take away his cancer
For I know your love, oh Lord.
A love that has set me free.
Grant me this one small request
Because he's more than a friend.
He's like a brother to me.
We have shared life's ups and downs.
Some with laughter some with tears.
Friends for oh so many years.
His folks always treated me like their very own—
Something I will never forget.
I gave my life to you, oh Lord,
So could you give one small thing back.
Take away his cancer.
If you must give it to someone,
Then give it to me.

Waiting

Here I sit another night staring at this screen,
Wondering if you might be staring back at me.
I look for words every day,
But they never seem to come.
Sitting here alone again isn't very much fun.
The words go out but don't come back.
I don't know what to do.
For I find comfort in your words
Because what you write is so true.
Oh, Lord, won't you write me back?
I'm waiting to hear from you.

Black and White

Life was better in black and white,
Long before they had color TV.
Most people knew right from wrong,
A sense of togetherness that made the family strong.
People cared about each other,
Giving a helping hand.
Now it's what can you give me,
To hell with you, I don't give a damn.
Oh, give me back the smell of spray starch,
Cooling down on a hot day in front of a fan.
Work might have been a whole lot harder,
But the company treated you more like a man,
Not just some number.
Friends got together for a little penny poker.

Now there is no time for one another.
We only have time for number one.
Oh, take me back to those black and white days,
When life was a whole lot better.

Forever Seventeen

Funny as it may seem,
I feel forever seventeen.
Never feeling my age,
Maybe it's just a stage
I seem to never have outgrown.
Now fifty has come and gone.
I wonder what went wrong,
Why I don't think like old people do.
I make fun of life people say,
Just like back in the day.
For I can find something funny in what people say.
Or maybe it's just a way
I try to remove people's pain.
For without laughter we grow old
All too soon.

Time Machine

Look out the windshield and see the future.
Gaze into the rearview mirror, and you see the past.
Look to the side, and there is the present.
All this from the seat of your car.

True Love Is

True love is found by giving away your heart,
Time after time,
Until it comes back unbroken.

The Greatest Surgeon

The greatest surgeon on earth
Cannot match the tender touch
Of the person
Who can mend a broken heart.

Forgiveness

Lord, soften my heart
So I may see
That without him
There wouldn't be me.
I know what he's done
Hurt more than just me.
But you, my Lord, are the judge,
Not lowly me.
For in you I find my strength.
So I cannot let what he did harden my heart.
If I do, your glory will never come to me.
For you forgave the world
After what we did to you.
So let me forgive.
For I want to be just like you.

God's Given Me Two

Two eyes to see when you are hurting.
Two lips so I can talk with you when you are lonely.
Two ears so I can sit and listen to you when no one
Else seems to care anymore.
Two arms to wrap around you when you need
Comforting.
Two hands so I can help you do things you are no
Longer able to do.
Two legs so I can come to you in your time of
Need.
Two feet so I can follow you when you need
Someone by your side.
But only one heart for that's all I need to
Share my love with the world.

Never Let

Never let a mirror steal your youth.
For true age is reflected in your
Mind, heart, and soul.

Love Echoes

True love is like an echo.
Once it is given out,
It is returned again and again …
Forever.

Life Seasons

Having known you in the spring of my life
Reminds me of the summer giving up her last breath,
Before it's sudden end,
Giving way to fall and her chilly greeting
Of what is on the way.
But those memories of you will forever keep my heart warm
In the winters of my life.

My Goal

Though I now walk the earth,
My goal is to walk with the angels.

For Me

In you I find peace,
A safe place to be
When the world is going crazy.
I know you're with me
For you are the rock,
The rock that stands against the raging sea.
You gave me a purpose
In what I was to be.
When I was captured by life's troubles,
You set me free.
I am starting to see my part.
To help all who come my way.
The ones who are in need the most.
To feel your healing heart
Now the life I know
Is to give my life to thee.
For you, my Lord,
Stretched out your arms on the cross for me.

Believe

When there's no one to turn to, turn to me.
When there's no one to call for help, you can call on me.
When you think you are lost, follow me.
When you think things are hopeless, hope in me.
When life's burdens become too great, I will set you free.
For everything is possible if you believe in me.

GPS

On the road of life,
God is my GPS.

When We Were Young

After all these years I can't let go
Of a feeling I felt long ago
When I was so very young.
I guess because back in those days
Happiness lasted for more than one day.
I believed that dreams could come true.
Now that that I am getting old,
Seeing how the world can be so cold,
It's amazing how friends from so long ago
Can warm my frozen heart.
They bring back memories of yesterday,
Bringing back hope for better days.
Oh, how much wiser we were
When we were so young.

Look in the Mirror

Look in the mirror and you will see
The person in the mirror
Is a lot like me,
Hearing about your life and who you turned out to be.
Sometimes it sounds you're talking not about you,
But you're talking about me.
Funny how alike we are in so many ways.
Too bad we didn't see it back in the old days.
Maybe we could have bypassed some of the pain.
I used to pray the Lord is my shepherd and didn't know why.
You opened my eyes
To see that I was always part of his flock.
For You are my blessing and *you* are my rock.

Temptress

Loneliness is my temptress.
She calls me by name,
Asking me to do evil
Against my Lord and King.
As I sit here and ponder
Which way will I go,
I hear the Lord calling me.
For he never leaves me alone.
So I just turn around, and there he is
Standing next to me.
Even when I wander from him,
He'll never wander from me.

No Plan

I still dream about tomorrow.
Remember yesterday.
Live every moment.
For today may be my last day.
I don't plan for the future
For it may never come.
But I never waste a moment
For there is too much work to be done
To try and make this world a better place
For future generations to come,
To spread the word of Jesus Christ
So all will understand
That he will take care of everything
Both here and in the promised land.
All you have to do is believe in him,
Putting your life in his hands.

My Cousin and Me

You're more than a cousin to me.
All these years you've been a big part of me.
God's made us closer than most, and I thank him of course.
For without you I might not be me.
For you've always been there,
Showing me how much you care
When life's not been very kind to me.
So I hope and I pray that God blesses you every day.
The way you've been a blessing to me.

Shadow Caster

Do not walk in the shadow of others,
But become the shadow caster.

One of a Kind

All I have to do is close my eyes
To have you materialize.
I know it's been such a long time
From the last time we stood side by side.
But time stands still inside of me.
So today how we look doesn't mean that much to me
For the person inside is what matters most.
Time can never change what's inside, you see,
Unless we let go of who we want to be.
For the Lord has given me back my sight
To see his power and feel his might.
So I can see into people's hearts.
All I can feel is good in you,
In everything you say and what you do.
You are so very rare in this world today.
I thank the Lord for having you come my way.

We All

I believe that we all fall in love.
Sometimes that love lasts forever.
They may become our husbands or our wives.
Or just a memory that never seems to fade.
It lives in a place we go to
Every now and then when life seems to be too much
To put back the smile that was once upon our faces.

The Lord Is Coming

The Lord is coming people.
He's coming to set us free.
The Lord is coming people
To end this misery.
The Lord is coming people
So all may believe
That he still loves us people
For all eternity.
Why can't you see this people.
Open your eyes, and you will see
The Lord is coming people,
For you and me.

A Song

Funny how your life can be written in a song,
Turning on the radio just to sing along.
Suddenly you realize what they are singing about
Is all about you.
If you listen to Rascal Flatts everyday,
You think they were singing about us two.